The B

Odyssey

Jack Lohrke - Volume I

James Francis McGee

Small Miracles Publishing Company >>>

First edition 2020

(Cover Photo: Jack "Lucky" Lohrke, New York Giants, 1947)

"…Knowing how swiftly all the years go by,

Where dawn and sunset blend in one brief sky."

- Grantland Rice, 1954

"Optimism is the faith that leads to achievement." **- Helen Keller**

For the love of my life, Kristina!

"The only real game, I think, in the world is baseball." - Babe Ruth

Table of Contents

1. The Greatest Game Ever Invented
2. The Struggles of the Seventies
3. The Magical Year
4. Jack "Lucky" Lohrke
5. From Pasadena to Twin Falls
6. From the Ballpark to the Battlefield
7. The Spokane Indians
8. A Star of the Coast League
9. Boston Calling
10. Major League Rookie
11. 1948, A Season of Change
12. A Trip to Jersey City and the Big Screen
13. Pitching and Playing in 1950
14. From St. Petersburg to the World Series
15. The City of Brotherly Love
16. From Pennsylvania to Maryland and Back
17. A Pirate and Then a Star
18. An All-Star Season in South America
19. Go North Young Man
20. The Last Innings
21. Seasons of Security
22. Honors and Recognition
23. The Greatest Reunion of the Greatest Team
24. A Return to the Diamond

1

The Greatest Game Ever Invented

In 1970, I loved the San Francisco Giants baseball club. My dad was a big Giants fan and he would take my brothers and I on long treks, which involved two buses and lots of patience, from Alameda to Candlestick Park. We marveled at the players for the orange and black such as Willie Mays, Willie McCovey, Chris Speier, and Bobby Bonds. At the young age of six, I decided that I wanted to be a baseball player.

Later that year, my parents signed me up to play baseball with the Lincoln Lions, a t-shirt league park and rec team. We hit balls off of a skinny black tee and ran around chaotically on the verdant outfield grass. I only remember one teammate on that 1970 Lions team, a dark-haired dynamo named Ricky Young, who would go on to become a national champion wrestler in his teen years. This kid ran fast, hit the ball hard, and threw far!

For some reason, my family wasn't able to sign me up for park league baseball after that exciting season at Lincoln Park. I kept in "baseball" shape by throwing a tennis ball against our front concrete steps and fielding the rebound time and time again. Once in a while, the kids in my neighborhood would go to Krusi Park with green Oakland A's giveaway bats and rubber-hard balls. I joined them every so often, bringing my small and stiff Rico Petrocelli mitt with me.

2

The Struggles of the Seventies

In 1971, the Giants won the National League western division title with manager Charlie Fox at the helm. I was in second grade now, at St. Philip Neri Catholic School, trying to make my way through the class work as I had baseball on my mind. One of our wonderful teachers at SPN was Sister Dennis Marie, a tall, kind nun who just happened to love the Giants, too. (She even had an SF Giants wastebasket in her room!)

The next year, our neighborhood friends who were A's fans were in for a treat as Oakland shockingly won the World Series. I told them time and time again that the Giants were still better. In '73, those darn A's won the Series again and I went right on defending my beloved Giants. It got very exasperating the next year as the Athletics won a third straight series title. (The Auen boys from across the street went to a series game that year and stormed the field with thousands of A's fans. They ended up bringing home a patch of sod they tore from the Coliseum outfield. Their mom planted that small section of grass in their front yard, where it lived for over twenty years!)

I grew up a bit over those few years and in fourth grade I had my big chance, a tryout for the St. Philip Neri Spartans CYO baseball team! I could catch and throw well, so I tried out for an outfield position. My hitting wasn't too good, but I worked hard and hoped for the best.

After a week of tryouts, my name wasn't on the posted list, and I was very sad. I tried to make our SPN school team again in 1975, 1976, and 1977, but to no avail. I was cut every year and did my best to soothe my ego by playing my second favorite sport for the Spartans, basketball.

The 1977 team was a dynamic group of ball players who went on to win the East Bay Catholic Youth League championship. Pitchers JoJo Perri, Rich Bullock, and Big John Bennett led the way. John Crestetto, Morris Gustin, Rich Wendling, Mike Brannan, Jim Kenyon, and the other kids hit and ran to many wins. I was happy for the guys as they won game after game.

In eighth grade, I was taller and smarter and looking to finally make our baseball squad, but it wasn't meant to be. We were saddened to learn that SPN wouldn't have baseball in 1978, instead a softball team was fielded. I put my mitt on the shelf, started lifting weights at Johnny's Gym, and looked ahead to Alameda High School's Thompson Field for a transition from the diamond to the gridiron.

3

The Magical Year

For the next thirteen years, I missed baseball, never truly forgetting my first athletic love, but then...

In 1991, I experienced the most magical year ever as I met my future bride, Kristina Lohrke, and through her I was able to rekindle my love of the greatest game ever invented! Kristina was a huge San Francisco Giants fan! In fact, I learned that her dad, Jack Lohrke, had played for the Giants when they ruled the Polo Grounds in New York.

Kristina and I went to our first game together at Candlestick Park in the fall, my first Giants game since I was a fourth grader. I felt like I was back home, and I cheered and smiled and shed tears of baseball joy! I was back!!!

4

Jack "Lucky" Lohrke

Jack was born in Los Angeles in 1924 and later attended Southgate High School. He wasn't able to play high school sports because his hardworking parents required that he help out at home after school and work as soon as possible to help with the family finances.

Jack and his two brothers, Kenny and Bob, kept active and fit as they helped their parents work picking fruit in the warm Southern California orchards. Jack's first real job was at the Vogue movie theatre in Southgate, working on a ladder replacing light bulbs on the theatre's marquee.

VOGUE
CARLISLE
MARY CARLISLE IN CHAMPAGNE
JACK HOLT IN

5

From Pasadena to Twin Falls

In the spring of 1942, Jack was finally able to find time to play organized baseball. The Pasadena Dons, a local semi-pro team, was the club he latched on with, and it was there that Jack met a tall, scrappy first baseman named Nick Sunseri. The two hit it off and shortly thereafter Jack was introduced to Nick's lovely sister, Marie, who would later become his bride of more than sixty years.

Jack Lohrke, Pasadena Dons, 1942

Jack was a standout infielder for the Pasadena team in ‘42 and caught the attention of professional scouts from the Pacific Coast League’s San Diego Padres. Before he knew it, Jack was signed to a pro contract with San Diego.

Jack and another young player, Dell Oliver, impressed Padres manager Cedric Durst during the brief Coast League exhibition season. Oliver was a pitcher who had played with Ted Williams at San Diego’s Hoover High School. Shortly thereafter, Dell was drafted into the United States Air Force and he ended up flying fifty missions as a gunner on a B17 bomber. Oliver never again played pro baseball as he injured his arm while playing for the Air Force baseball team in Texas after returning from the War.

Cedric Durst (L) and the legendary Frankie Frisch

Jack Lohrke ended up taking over third base while regular Art Garibaldi argued salary terms with the front office (Brandes/Swank.) When the garrulous Garibaldi returned to the field, Manager Durst decided to send Jack down to San Diego's Northwest affiliate in Idaho, the Twin Falls Cowboys, to gain more experience.

A month later, Jack was back in San Diego to play seventeen games for the Padres when Garibaldi injured himself. Lohrke received much praise for helping bring the team together (Brandes/Swank.) During his short stint, Jack played third and also was used as a relief pitcher, giving up only two hits to seventeen batters.

Jack returned to Twin Falls in early May and played so well for the Cowboys, batting .271 and ruling the infield, that he was named the team's Most Valuable Player at the end of the season!

LKCA

6

From the Ballpark to the Battlefield

The future looked bright for this phenomenal baseball talent, but the world stage had other ideas as Jack was drafted into the United States Army in 1943 to fight in World War II. Jack participated in the rigors of basic training in North Carolina. His regiment was slated to be a part of Operation Overlord, also known as the "D-Day invasion."

Sure enough, Jack and his military brothers were secretly sent across the English Channel and in the early morning hours of June 6, 1944, Jack landed in the middle of the hell that was Omaha Beach. The battle was horrific as countless allied troops were killed or wounded, some to the left and right of Jack, as he bravely made his way up the beach under heavy fire. The Nazis were beaten back eventually and General Eisenhower's men had gained a momentous foothold as the tide of the War was shifted.

Later in the year, Jack also fought valiantly in the Battle of the Bulge. At one point during the frigid winter war time, he was so cold and tired that he fell asleep standing up next to a haystack. Jack's military service lasted from 1943 through the end of the war in 1945. He bid farewell to the European continent and was shipped back across the Atlantic on a troop transport ship.

Jack ended up in New Jersey, awaiting a military flight back to Los Angeles. His spot on the plane was set until minutes before the plane took off. A high ranking army officer needed to be added to the flight, so Jack was bumped for a later departure. As fate would have it, the plane crashed shortly after takeoff and all on board were killed. Private Lohrke's life had been spared, just as it had been on the sands of Normandy.

7

The Spokane Indians

Jack returned to LA, and the San Diego Padres came calling once again at the start of the 1946 baseball season. Pepper Martin was the new manager for the Padres and he decided to assign the 22 year old infielder, along with Padres teammate Garry Nelson, to the Western International League to start the season. The two talented baseball men would be playing for the Spokane Indians club. (The Indians were a noteworthy team in part since Bing Crosby was one of their owners.)

Dad, Southgate High School (1942)

The young, and possibly rusty, Jack Wayne Lohrke didn't miss a beat as he fielded, threw, and slugged his way to a team high .345 batting average for Spokane. The Padres brass down in San Diego decided to recall Jack to the Coast League club and on June 24th they made their move. A telegram was sent to the talented in-fielder, but the Indians had already left on their bus, heading to Bremerton on a cold and rainy night.

The team bus pulled over at a roadside diner prior to making its way up the stormy mountain by way of Snoqualmie Pass and then Bremerton. The players chatted and ate hamburgers as a lone highway patrolman entered the diner, looking for Jack to hand him the Padre's wire. Lohrke thanked the officer, read the telegram, and bid his teammates farewell, planning on hitchhiking back to Spokane.

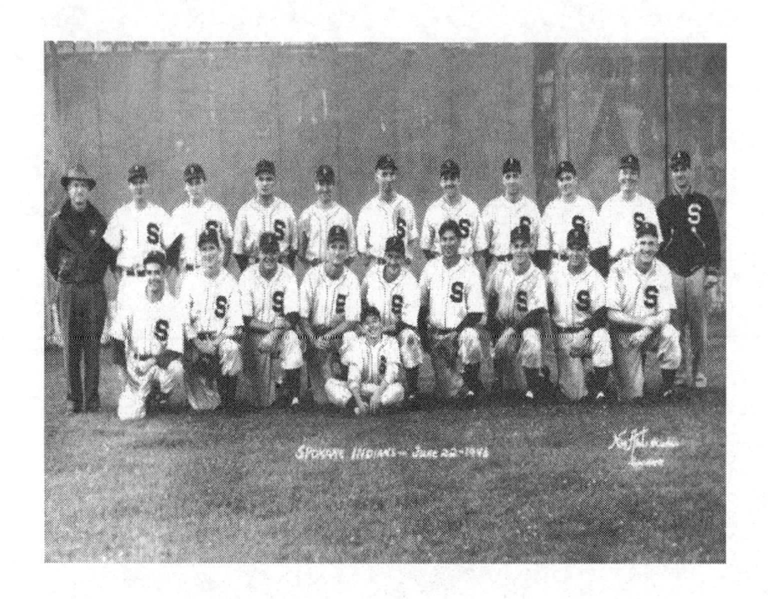

The Indian players boarded their motor coach and looked forward to some shut eye on the final leg of their trip. (They were to play a game the next day.) Tragically, the bus would never arrive at its destination as the driver swerved to avoid a black sedan that had crossed over into his lane, causing the bus to slide in the storm and crash over the side of the highway. It tore up over a hundred feet of guardrail and then plummeted down the stormy embankment and burst into flames. Nine young players would lose their lives in one of the worst sports tragedies of all time.

Since Jack had cheated death once again, the press dubbed him "Lucky" Lohrke, a name he never was comfortable with.

8

A Star of the Coast League

Dad and Padres Manager Pepper Martin

For the remainder of the 1946 baseball season, Jack played second base and shortstop for the Padres with Pepper Martin at the helm. San Diego was undergoing a tumultuous season with numerous injuries, trades, and lineup changes. There were rumblings that some players were dissatisfied with Manager Martin's leadership. Lohrke persevered through the San Diego storm of a season and by mid-August was batting .331.

A local newspaper reported on August 24th that baseball rumors had Jack "Lucky" Lohrke sold for 1947 delivery to the Pittsburgh Pirates for a price of $15,000 and three players (Brandes/Swank.) No less than five major league teams had been reported bidding for Jack, although the Pirate rumor was unfounded and never came to fruition.

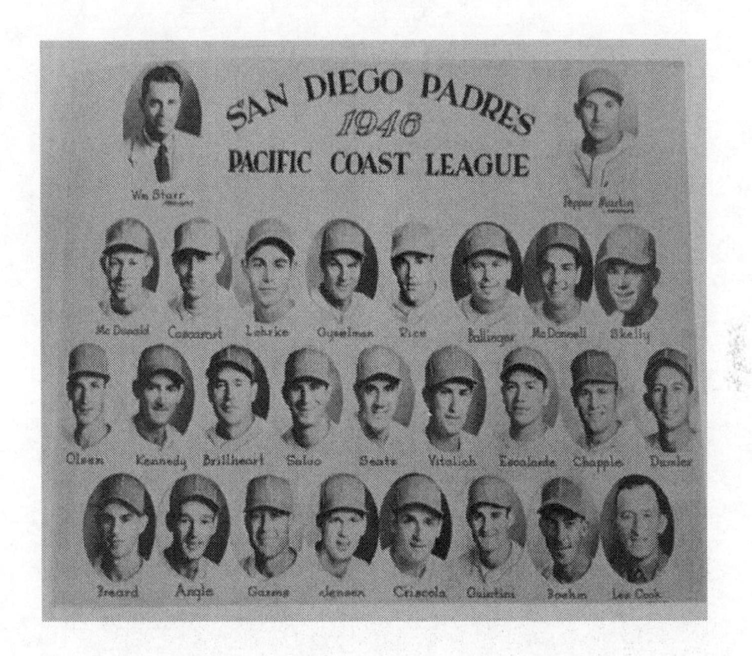

The '46 Padres further faltered on the field as they dropped more than half of their last fifty games of the season. Lohrke continued to be a steadying force in the infield and for the team, gaining some much needed experience and finishing the year batting over .300. Jack was selected to the Coast League All-Star team along with San Diego players Al Olsen and Dick Gyselman. In August, the All-Stars played the league leading San Francisco Seals, a fabulous team whose roster included Sal Taormina, Larry Jansen, Ferris Fain, and Vince DiMaggio.

The handsome Jack Lohrke (1946)

The twenty-two year old Jack Lohrke looked forward to what life would bring as the first year after World War II moved to a close. Only time would tell…

9

Boston Calling

In August of 1946, Jack was selected in the first round of the Rule V draft by Major League Baseball's Boston Braves. The team had high hopes for the baseball phenom, but shortly thereafter, the New York Giants ball club did some backroom maneuvering to steal away Lohrke from Boston.

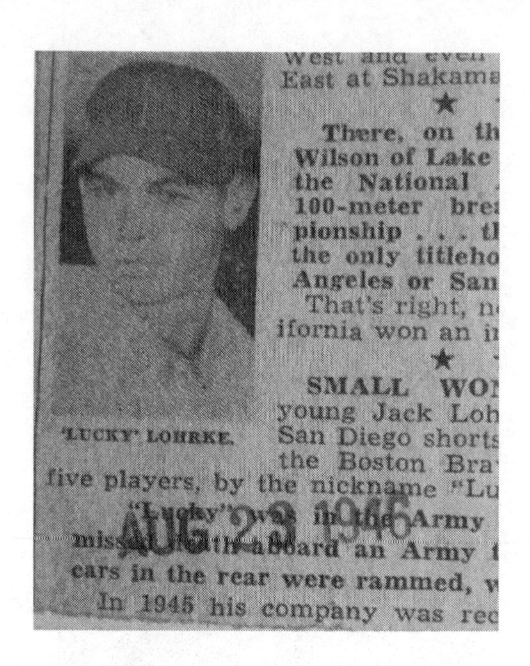

West and even
East at Shakama

★

There, on th
Wilson of Lake
the National
100-meter bre
pionship . . . t
the only titleho
Angeles or San
That's right, n
ifornia won an i

★

SMALL WO
young Jack Loh
San Diego shorts
the Boston Bra
five players, by the nickname "Lu
"Lucky" was in the Army
missed death aboard an Army t
cars in the rear were rammed, w
In 1945 his company was rec

'LUCKY' LOHRKE.

AUG 23 1946

The Braves cried foul and Commissioner A.B. "Happy" Chandler intervened, deciding that the Giants could keep Lucky Lohrke, but New York needed to send five players to Boston as compensation.

10

Major League Rookie

Around the same time that the Giants and Braves were wrestling over the rights to Jack, another young star from the Pacific Coast League was signed by New York. Larry Jansen, an amazing pitcher who had won thirty games during the 1946 campaign for the San Francisco Seals, was inked by New York to a Major League contract. Larry and Jack, along with Bobby Thomson and Carroll "Whitey" Lockman, would become a youthful nucleus to the fortunes of the Giants during the '47 baseball run.

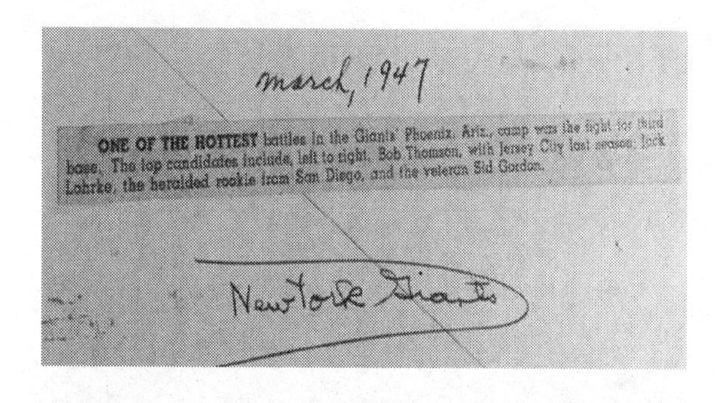
march, 1947

ONE OF THE HOTTEST battles in the Giants' Phoenix, Ariz., camp was the fight for third base. The top candidates include, left to right, Bob Thomson, with Jersey City last season; Jack Lohrke, the heralded rookie from San Diego, and the veteran Sid Gordon.

New York Giants

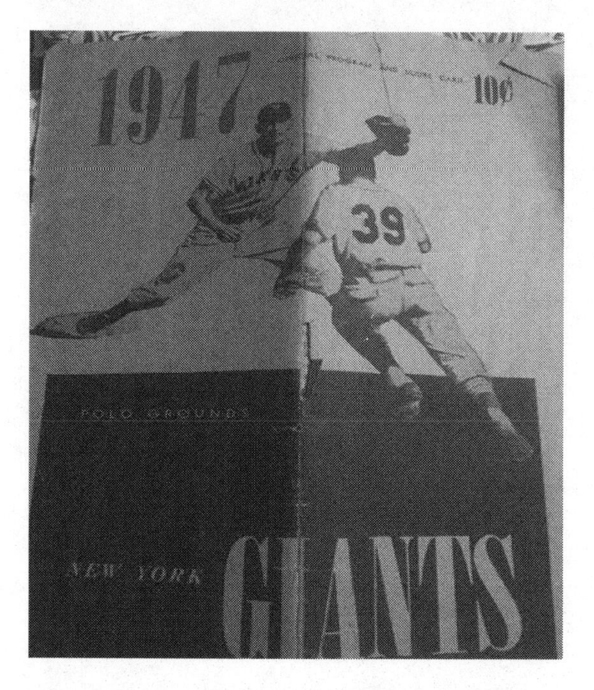

"One of (the New Yorker) magazine's treasures, E.B. White, would soon write,'No one should come to New York to live unless he is willing to be lucky'" (New York 2019). Jack Lohrke and his Giant teammates certainly came to New York willing to live and win!

Spring training rolled around and Jack was off to Arizona where he trained and played impressive ball for New York. His bat was powerful and quick, his arm was live, and his fast feet were said to be the speediest on the team.

Jack soon became fast friends with Larry and Whitey. In fact, Jack and Whitey were roommates in a small apartment in New York close by the train tracks. Their strong friendship would endure for over six decades.

Larry Jansen

Carroll "Whitey" Lockman

INFIELDERS		
Blattner, Robert	27	St. Louis, Mo.
Kerr, John	24	New York, N. Y.
Lajeskie, Richard	21	Passaic, N. J.
Lohrke, Jack	22	Bell, Cal.
Mize, John	34	St. Louis, Mo.
Rigney, William	27	Oakland, Cal.
Thomson, Robert	23	Staten Island, N. Y.
Witek, Nicholas	31	Luzerne, Pa.
Young, Norman	31	New York, N. Y.

1947 New York Giants Spring Training Infield Prospects

1947 was a landmark year in the Major Leagues as Jackie Robinson broke the color barrier when he debuted with the Dodgers of Brooklyn in April. That same month, Jack Lohrke began his MLB career with Brooklyn's nemesis, the New York "Baseball" Giants.

The Dodgers' amazing Jackie Robinson

Jack and Marie dated whenever Jack could make it back to the West Coast, spending time at movie theatres and restaurants. They were a wonderful couple who had dreams for the future. Marie Sunseri worked as a telephone switchboard operator for a time in LA, after spending a year at Compton Junior College.

Jack Lohrke and Marie Sunseri (1947)

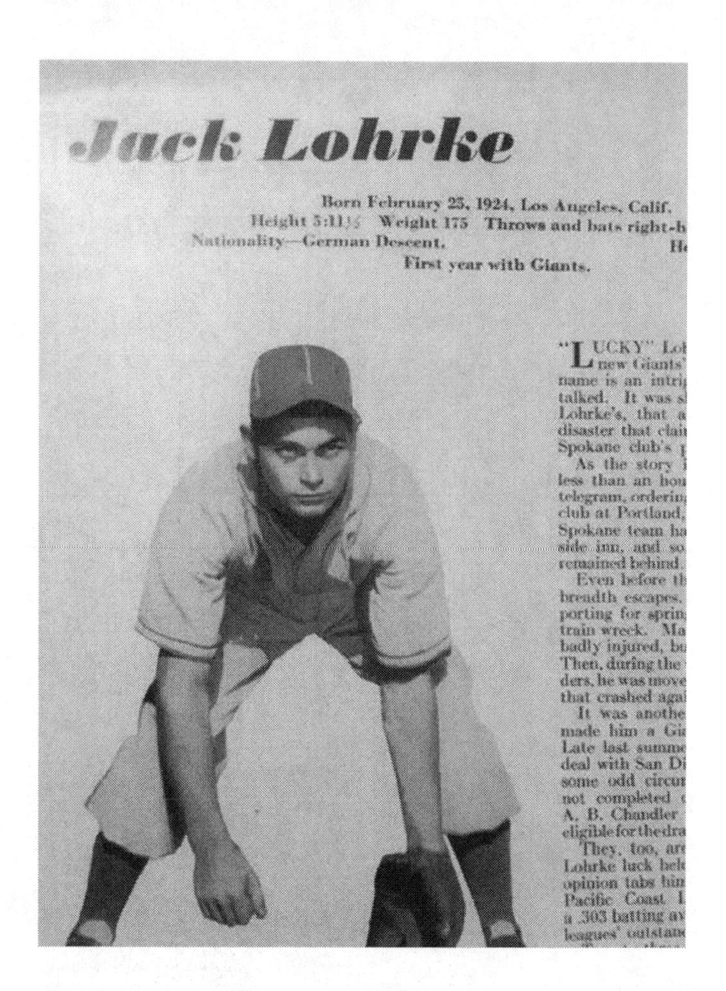
Jack Lohrke

Born February 25, 1924, Los Angeles, Calif.
Height 5:11½ Weight 175 Throws and bats right-h
Nationality—German Descent.
First year with Giants.

"LUCKY" Lo
new Giants'
name is an intri
talked. It was s
Lohrke's, that a
disaster that clai
Spokane club's
As the story
less than an hou
telegram, orderin
club at Portland,
Spokane team ha
side inn, and so
remained behind.
Even before th
breadth escapes,
porting for sprin
train wreck. Ma
badly injured, bu
Then, during the
ders, he was move
that crashed aga
It was anothe
made him a Gi
Late last summe
deal with San Di
some odd circu
not completed
A. B. Chandler
eligible for the dra
They, too, ar
Lohrke luck hel
opinion tabs hin
Pacific Coast L
a .303 batting av
leagues' outstan

The manager for New York in '47 was the legendary Hall of Famer, Mel Ott, an incredible ball player who had clubbed 511 home runs during his long and prestigious career. Ott loved Jack's talent and tenacity, having so much faith in Lohrke that he named him the Giants regular third baseman at the season's onset.

Mel Ott

The Polo Grounds

Jack made his major league debut at the start of the 1947 season in April playing third base. He clubbed a single in his first major league at bat, a loud shot off Dodger pitcher Vic Lombardi. Unfortunately, Jack was caught stealing moments later. The talented infielder played the vast majority of the games for the Giants that year as the third sacker. Lohrke blasted "his first major league home run on June 9th at the Polo Grounds against the Pittsburgh Pirates' Kirby Higbe" (SABR).

Lucky Lohrke (7-23-47)

"LUCKY" Lohrke is what they call him, the new Giants' infielder, and his right to the name is an intriguing tale wherever baseball is talked. It was sheer fortune, or the luck that is Lohrke's, that allowed him to escape the bus disaster that claimed the lives of so many of the Spokane club's players last summer.

As the story is told Lohrke got off the bus less than an hour before the fatal accident. A telegram, ordering him to report to the San Diego club at Portland, caught up with him just as the Spokane team had stopped for dinner at a roadside inn, and so, as the bus drove on, Lohrke remained behind.

Even before that he had a reputation for hair breadth escapes. Early in his career, while reporting for spring training he was involved in a train wreck. Many of the train's passengers were badly injured, but he emerged without a scratch. Then, during the war, when travelling on Army orders, he was moved by "brass" priority from a plane that crashed against a California mountain peak.

It was another strange quirk of fortune that made him a Giant instead of a Boston Brave. Late last summer the Boston club negotiated a deal with San Diego for his services, but through some odd circumstance the commitments were not completed on schedule, and Commissioner A. B. Chandler ruled that Lohrke must become eligible for the draft, whence the Giants claimed him.

They, too, are under the impression that the Lohrke luck held for them, since all professional opinion tabs him as the finest of the recent year Pacific Coast League propects. He compiled a .303 batting average for San Diego, and was the leagues' outstanding shortstop.

Twenty-three years old Lohrke resides with

Jack impressed Manager Mel Ott during the '47 campaign as he stole bases, played a solid third, and crushed the ball over the outfield fences twelve times. The only issue was Lohrke's cannon of a right arm was so strong that often-times NY first sacker Johnny "Big Cat" Mize had trouble catching Jack's laser throws to first. Years later, Whitey Lockman recounted, "Unfortunately, the official scorers usually gave Jack the errors, rather than list them on Mize's stats since he was the veteran."

Johnny "Big Cat" Mize

One of Lohrke's most memorable moments came on a cool afternoon at Forbes Field, home to the Pittsburgh Pirates. Jack and Wes Westrum were warming up before batting practice when Wes asked Jack, "Hey, do you know who that is sitting over there?" Jack looked up and saw an older gentleman sitting on a wooden chair, leaning back against a wall.

"Who?" Jack responded.

"That's Honus Wagner!" responded Westrum. The two young players walked over and met the immortal Mr. Wagner, shaking his still strong right hand.

Honus Wagner

The Giants' play in 1947 was inconsistent, in great part due to some pitching and defensive shortcomings. The bright light that year was batting power that blasted numerous home runs by many of the New York players including Mize, Willard Marshall, Al Dark, and Jack.

In fact, as the season neared its conclusion, the Giants were on the cusp of shattering the Major League Baseball team record for homers held by the 1936 Yankees "Murderers' Row" of Babe Ruth and Lou Gehrig. The record stood at 182 homeruns, but as the Giants were preparing for a game with the Boston Braves, they had 181.

Lucky Lohrke getting ready to club a homer

The media and many New York fans, including Johnny Mize's wife, were confident the record would be broken by the "Big Cat." Mize had belted fifty homers in '47, so he was the player most likely to club the clouts to tie and break the Yankees hallowed record. But that was not meant to be, as Lucky Lohrke smashed a homer at Braves Field on Labor Day with over 43,000 fans in attendance to break the mark.

Braves Field

Jack after breaking the Major League homerun record

11

1948, A Season of Change

Jack's 1948 Topps card

Jack looked forward to building upon the successes of his rookie season in 1948. Unfortunately, a managerial change in mid season, replacing the beloved Mel Ott with former Dodger manager Leo Durocher, would send Lohrke's baseball career in a different direction.

Durocher was a gritty manager who had been a scrappy player and he wanted to bring in his own type of players to the New York team. Leo made changes to the Giants club that included replacing Jack as the team's third sacker with Sid Gordon, who ended up having a career year with thirty homers. Jack's role was changed to a utility player where he played second, short, and third base, depending on the need.

GIANTS

jottings

Volume XIV, No. 1 MARCH 1, 1948 New York City, N. Y.

Jack Lohrke

1948 Giants Jottings with Jack and the "Big Cat"

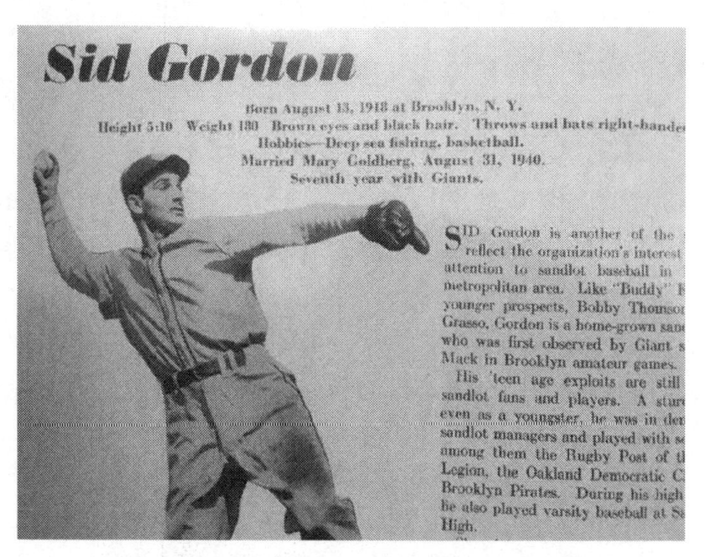

Sid Gordon

Born August 13, 1918 at Brooklyn, N. Y.
Height 5:10 Weight 180 Brown eyes and black hair. Throws and bats right-hande
Hobbies—Deep sea fishing, basketball.
Married Mary Goldberg, August 31, 1940.
Seventh year with Giants.

SID Gordon is another of the
reflect the organization's interest
attention to sandlot baseball in
metropolitan area. Like "Buddy" K
younger prospects, Bobby Thomso
Grasso, Gordon is a home-grown san
who was first observed by Giant s
Mack in Brooklyn amateur games.

His 'teen age exploits are still
sandlot fans and players. A stur
even as a youngster, he was in de
sandlot managers and played with s
among them the Rugby Post of t
Legion, the Oakland Democratic C
Brooklyn Pirates. During his high
he also played varsity baseball at S
High.

Sid Gordon, a fine person and player

Manager Durocher pushed and bellowed his way into his new leadership position, shaking things up on the Giants roster and in their club-house. The manager's strong persona did little to improve the team's final place in the standings as New York finished 1948 in fifth place, thirteen games behind the pennant winning Boston Braves, the team who had drafted Jack the year before.

Despite the tumultuous '48 season having its low points for Jack, he was still a major leaguer in the greatest city in the world. Along the way he met many legends of sports and the entertainment world such as Hall of Famer Christy Mathewson's battery mate, Chief Meyers, and Hollywood film stars Bud Abbott and Lou Costello. On one night in 1948, Jack, Whitey, and a few other teammates got to sit ringside during a boxing match at the hallowed Madison Square Garden with the world famous comedy team.

Dad and teammates with Abbott and Costello at Madison Square Garden in 1948

By far the high point of 1948 for the twenty-four year old Lohrke was December 10th, when he married the love of his life, Marie Josephine Sunseri, back home in Los Angeles. The young couple moved into a beautiful home in Downey, California and planned their dreams for the future.

The newlyweds, December, 1948

12

A Trip to Jersey City and the Big Screen

The 1949 baseball season for New York didn't go much better than '48 as the Giants finished in fifth place once again. Jack's time on the field was inconsistent at best, although when he did play, his results were solid. A thumb injury as well as an eye condition further made the 1949 campaign, challenging.

Jack stealing second base versus the Phillies at Shibe Park

In addition, the Giants' rivals, the Brooklyn Dodgers, and their phenomenal Negro League acquisition Jackie Robinson, were winning games at rapid rate. (The Dodgers ended up winning almost 100 games along with the National League pennant.)

NEW YORK GIANTS, 1949
Front row—Temasic, Fitzsimmons, coach; Marshall, Haas, Rigney, Higbe, Franks, coach; Gordon, Thomp-
on, Jones, Yvars. Back row—Shellenback, coach; Lafata, Williams, Zabala, Irvin, Milne, Westrum, Koslo, Kerr,
ansen, Hartung, Lohrke, Thomson, Lockman, Hansen, Mueller, Behrman, Bowman, Kress, coach; Rufer, Ken-
edy. Batboy Sterling in front.

1949 New York Giants

Leo Durocher sensed his plans weren't working out, even though he had changed coaches with the great Herman Franks coming on board, decided late in the year to add more players. Durocher tapped into the Negro Leagues in hopes of catch lightning in a bottle like Brooklyn did with Robinson.

The Giants signed third baseman Hank Thompson and outfielder Monte Irvin, two of the best of the best from the Negro Leagues. Thompson was a World War II veteran who was a star for the Kansas City Monarchs. Irvin was a thirty year old athlete who had starred in football for

Lincoln University in Missouri before serving our country in the War. Monte then played for the Newark Eagles in the Negro Leagues, earning all-star status more than once.

Hank Thompson

Hall of Famer, Monte Irvin

Irvin, who would go on to a Hall of Fame career for the Giants, and Thompson were much needed additions to the New York club. These new players limited Jack's game minutes further, and Leo Durocher decided to send Jack down to New York's AAA affiliate, the Jersey City Giants, so he could keep sharp. (There was talk in the media circles that the main reason Leo did not appreciate Jack's ability was that Lorraine Day, Durocher's Hollywood actress wife, was interested in the handsome Lohrke.)

In December of 1949, New York made a big trade as they sent Sid Gordon, Buddy Kerr, Wil- lard Marshall, and Red Webb to the Boston

Braves for infielders Eddie Stanky and Alvin Dark (Wikipedia.) Stanky, a scrappy player who drew numerous walks, had played for the Dodgers when Durocher was their manager. Dark was an outstanding shortstop who had been named Rookie of the Year in 1948 while playing for Boston. The two talented players were to become key pieces in the baseball machine that was being assembled with Leo at the helm.

Dad's 1949 Topps baseball card

Jack had one of his best seasons in his long baseball career in 1949 as he batted .267 with a .789 OPS while playing all over the infield for the Giants (SABR.) When Lucky was in Jersey City, he belted ten homers and batted an impressive .302. Jack forced the issue and made it hard for Durocher to keep him at the Triple A level for very long.

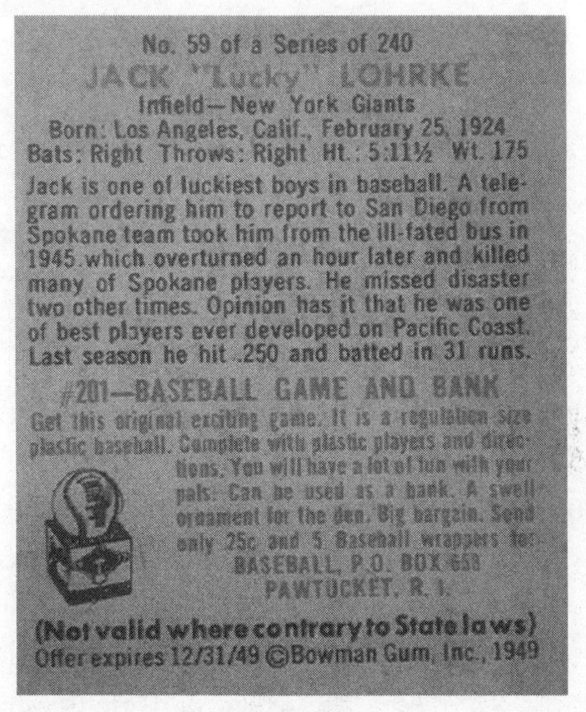

No. 59 of a Series of 240

JACK "Lucky" LOHRKE

Infield—New York Giants

Born: Los Angeles, Calif., February 25, 1924

Bats: Right Throws: Right Ht.: 5:11½ Wt. 175

Jack is one of luckiest boys in baseball. A telegram ordering him to report to San Diego from Spokane team took him from the ill-fated bus in 1945 which overturned an hour later and killed many of Spokane players. He missed disaster two other times. Opinion has it that he was one of best players ever developed on Pacific Coast. Last season he hit .250 and batted in 31 runs.

#201—BASEBALL GAME AND BANK

Get this original exciting game. It is a regulation size plastic baseball. Complete with plastic players and directions. You will have a lot of fun with your pals. Can be used as a bank. A swell ornament for the den. Big bargain. Send only 25c and 5 Baseball wrappers to:

BASEBALL, P.O. BOX 658

PAWTUCKET, R. I.

(Not valid where contrary to State laws)

Offer expires 12/31/49 ©Bowman Gum, Inc., 1949

1949 Topps

One of the highlights of the 1949 season was Jack's role in the Jimmy Stewart movie "The Stratton Story." Jack, along with a handful of pro ball players, were included in the Hollywood production about Monte Stratton, a major league pitcher who was injured during a hunting accident. He made his way back to pro ball wearing a prosthetic leg. (Jack can be seen playing shortstop in the film as well as walking past Stewart in one memorable scene.)

Jack signing a ball for actress June Allyson

Lohrke was brought back up to the New York squad later in the season where he saw limited time as a utility player at third, short, and second. The Giants coaching staff, among them Herman Franks, knew they needed to find a way to get the talented Lucky Lohrke on the field. There was even some talk of transitioning him to the New York bullpen since Jack's right arm was so electric. Only time would tell...

Jimmy Stewart and Frank Morgan

13

Pitching and Playing in 1950

Spring training in Arizona rolled around again for the next baseball season as Jack and Marie expected their first child, a boy who would be named Kurt. (Kurt would follow in his father's footsteps and play infield in the Boston Red Sox minor league system.) The happy couple was now living in Westchester, New York, during the season and returning to Los Angeles in the off season.

Jack working out as a pitcher, Spring Training, 1950

Franks and Durocher decided to test out Jack on the pitching mound during that 1950 spring training session. Lohrke impressed at times, but the team felt his talents playing the infield and being used as a pinch hitter and runner were more valuable in the short term.

More work on the pitching mound in Phoenix

This being Jack's fourth season in the big leagues was a crucial juncture in his pro ball career. Also, it was a big season for Manager Durocher, as it was his third year at the helm and he needed to keep the fans and management happy. Relegating Jack to the bullpen would lessen the time the fans could see him on the field, which might not help attendance as Jack was still a fan favorite. After it was all said and done, the 1950 campaign was fairly solid for the New York "Baseball" Giants as they battled to a third place finish in the National League, as Jack was used sparingly as a utility infielder, rarely seeing the pitching mound.

14

From St. Petersburg to the World Series

The 1951 New York Giants baseball season would be a season of change from start to finish. Spring training would be in St. Petersburg, Florida for the first time, as NY traded spring facilities with the Yankees.

Jack in Spring Training, St. Petersburg, Florida

Jack's name was once again in the headlines as he graced the footage of the 1951 Major League spring training baseball film's coverage of the New York Giants. Lohrke was filmed swinging the bat in the batting cage in Florida with the narrator's question of "who will play at third this year for the Giants, Jack "Lucky" Lohrke or Negro League star Hank Thompson." (Interestingly, when Jack was sent down to Jersey City, Hank took Jack's number, 16, and upon his return Lohrke now donned the number 17.)

The '51 season was up and down from the start, with the "Bums" from Brooklyn playing very well and eventually sitting atop the National League standings. The Giants added a few more players in 1951, including Negro League star Artie Wilson, who had once batted .400, and a twenty year old phenom named Willie Mays.

Artie Wilson with the Giants in 1951

Jack was still relegated to utility duty, although Durocher at least didn't send him back to Jersey City. By August, New York was reeling in the standings, trailing first place Brooklyn by 13 ½ games.

Things looked dismal until the Giants started to crush the ball and pitch extremely well, winning the vast majority of their remaining games along the way. (Interestingly, Leo Durocher tried to make a trade in August of ‘51 which would have sent Jack Lorhke and Bobby Thomson to the Chicago Cubs for outfielder Andy Pafko.)

NEW YORK GIANTS - NATIONAL LEAGUE CHAMPIONS - MIRACLE TEAM 1951
Giants

1951 New York “Baseball” Giants

The Dodgers heard the echoing footsteps of the Giants and by season’s end, the teams were tied atop the National League. A three game playoff was the next step to determine who would win the pennant and then face the marvelous New York Yankees in the World Series.

The teams split the first two games of the series and then history was set, as the Giants were ready to face the Dodgers on October 3, 1951 at the Polo Grounds in what would become one of the most famous baseball games of all time!

The Giants trailed late in the game by the score of 4 to 2 as millions of people watched the game on television (the first nationally televised baseball game in history!) Leading off the ninth frame saw New York's Alvin Dark slap a sharp single. Don "Mandrake" Mueller followed Dark with another single. Whitey Lockman then smashed a powerful double to score Al Dark cutting the Dodgers lead to just 4 to 3.

In a matter of minutes, the Giants were down to their last chance, as Brooklyn recorded two quick outs. Jack Lohrke was called on to start warming up since he would be coming into the game if it went into extra innings.

The “Scot”, Bobby Thomson, came up to bat to face Dodger pitcher Ralph Branca. As Jack readied himself to play in the tenth inning with the possibility of getting a game winning hit, Thomson belted a laser shot off a Branca pitch into the left field stands for the game winning homerun. This clout would be forever known as “The Shot Heard ‘Round the World” in baseball lore!

Bobby, Don, Durocher, Jack, and the rest of the Giants’ team stormed home plate and celebrated emphatically as the club had just punched its ticket to the Series!

Unfortunately, the Yankees ended up beating the Giants in the 1951 World Series 4 games to 2, to end the season on a down note. Jack was called upon to pinch hit twice in the Series as Joe DiMaggio played his last games with New York. Interestingly, Mickey Mantle was a rookie in '51 and he was just starting his fabled career as "Joltin' Joe" was just ending his. What would happen to Lucky Lohrke in 1952, his sixth season in the majors? Only time would tell…

15

The City of Brotherly Love

During the off-season, the Giants decided to get younger and that in part meant to trade Jack to another National League club, the Philadelphia Phillies. Lohrke's baseball odyssey had taken quite a few twists and turns from the semi-pro fields of Pasadena to southern Idaho to three years lost to military service to Spokane and San Diego and then to the Big Apple. Now, in Philly, Jack was starting a new baseball chapter with a new team and a new number, "lucky" number 7.

1952 Philadelphia Phillies

The Fightin' Phils were in an interesting place in 1952, being just two years removed from a World Series appearance. Future Hall of Fame pitcher Robin Roberts still graced the mound for the Phillies in '52, but the squad had lost some of its spark in the past few years. The fans in the "City of Brotherly Love" wanted a champion and never hesitated to shout and jeer their love and, at times, their disapproval.

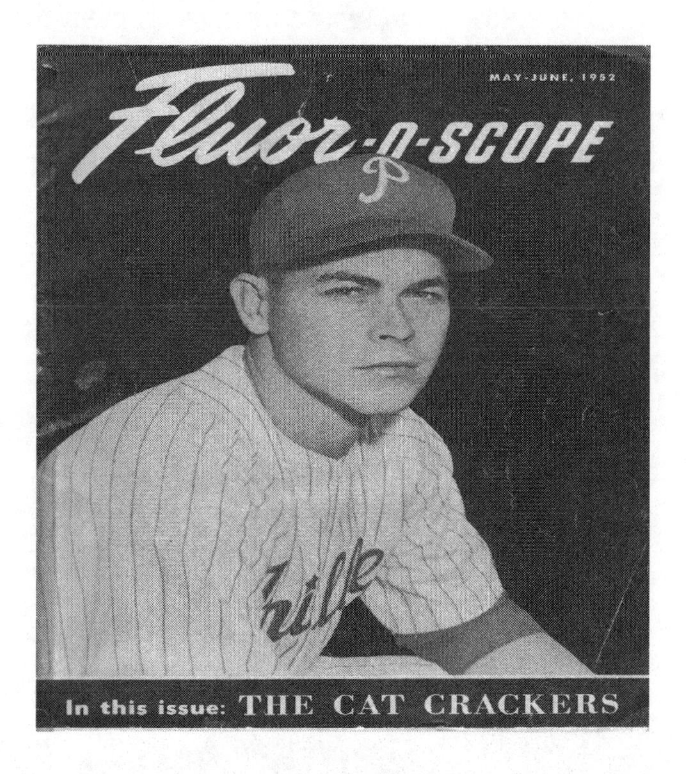

Jack's role with Philadelphia was to be that of a veteran utility player, although he hoped of course to make his way back to being a full time player once again. The red, white, and blue club had some fine moments in 1952, but failed to reach the hopes of its coaches and its fans, finishing in fourth place.

In 1952, Jack and Marie were blessed with a second child, Karen, in November, just about a month after season's end. The Lohrke's had a nice row house in Philly with a small patch of front lawn and a medium sized backyard. (Jack used to reminisce about how he had to carry their lawn-mower from the backyard through the house to the front lawn to cut his grass.) The young family wasn't sure what the upcoming chapter in Jack's baseball odyssey would bring…

16

From Pennsylvania to Maryland and Back

Seated in Front: Ken Rush --Batboy Jack Dunn--Batboy Ryan--2nd B
BACK ROW (right to left)- Roberts, P; Simmons, P; Torgeson, 1st B; Waitkus, 1st B; Lopata, C; Konstanty, P; Silvestri, Coach; Drews, P; Fox, P;
MIDDLE ROW (right to left)-Stuffel, P; Konstanty, P; Ashburn, CF; Nicholson, RF; Jones, 3rd B; Clark, OF; Miller, P; Ennis, LF; Burgess, C; Moyo [illegible]
OF; Weisher, Trainer
FRONT ROW (right to left)-Ridzik, P; Lohrke, LF; McDonnell, Coach; Wyrostek, RF; Glaviano, IF; Hamner, SS; Perkins, Coach; O'Neill, Mgr [illegible] E, Coach; Bengough, Coach; Hamner, P; Peterson, P

During the 1953 season with the Phillies, Jack battled injuries and saw his playing time limited even more. For the first time since 1949, Jack was once again moved down to Triple A, this time to play with the Phillies minor league affiliate the Baltimore Orioles.

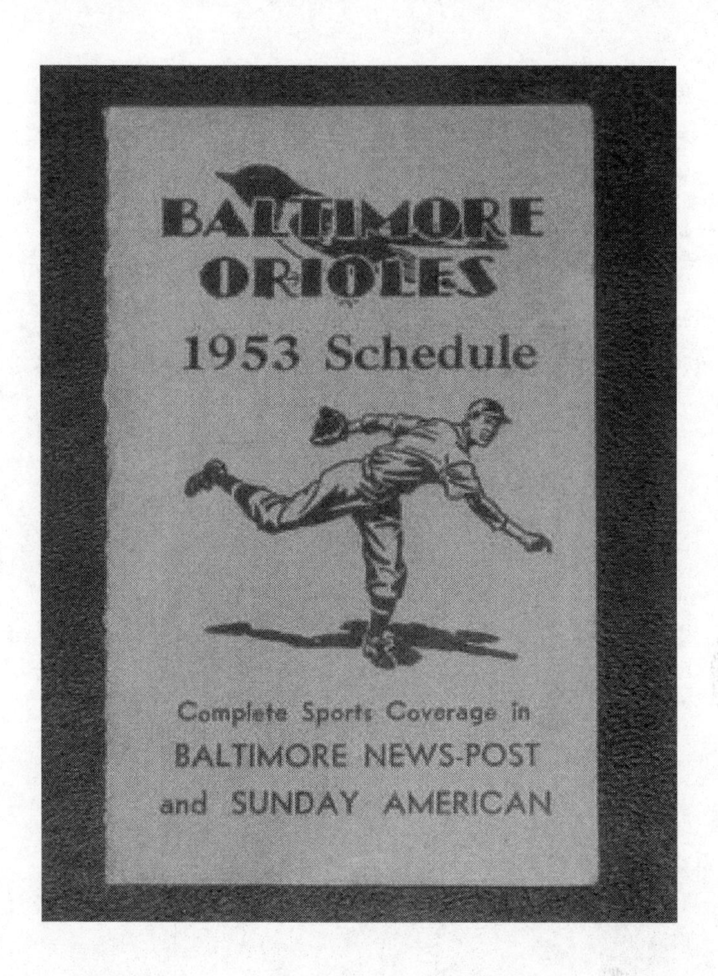

Now at twenty-nine years of age, and after playing eight years of pro ball after serving many harrowing months in Europe during World War II, Lohrke was starting to feel the effects of the physical wear and tear. Despite this challenge, Jack was recalled before season's end to rejoin the big club.

1953 Topps baseball card

17

A Pirate and Then a Star!

Jack turned thirty years old on February 25, 1954 and he soon found out that his next baseball chapter would begin with the Pirates of Pittsburgh. The Phils had traded Lucky to Pittsburgh for a veteran pitcher named Murray Dickson.

Jack Lohrke, Pittsburgh Pirate, 1954

Jack and the family were back in LA looking forward to a fresh start in spring training with the Pirates. (In 1952 and '53 the team held spring training in Havana, Cuba, but in 1954 Pittsburgh was slated to train on the "Treasure Coast" of Florida at Ft. Pierce.)

As it turned out, Jack would never don the black and gold colors of the Pirates during the regular season as the club sent him down before regular play began to the Hollywood Stars, an outstanding Pacific Coast League team that was the Pirates' top minor league squad. This was a surprise move, but it boded well for the Lohrke family as Jack would now be close to home.

1954 Hollywood Stars baseball club

Jack ended up playing solid ball for the Stars in 1954 and 1955. Hollywood ended the ‘54 season tied for first place in the Coast League and then dropped a few spots in the standings the following season.

The Stars’ management followed through with Leo Durocher’s bullpen experiment from 1950’s spring training and had Jack relief pitch on occasion. His ERA was in the low two’s as he impressed on the mound. In addition, Jack played third, second, and short during his stay with the Stars.

Jack arguing a call with umpire Emmett Ashford in 1954. Eleven years later, Ashford would break the color barrier and become the first African-American umpire in the Majors.

Jack and his five year old son, Kurt Lohrke, in 1955

Jack and Marie welcomed their third child into the family in February of 1955, a daughter named Kathy. Life was very busy for the Lohrkes as they made their home in Downey, California. At one point, the couple was invited to a party in Hollywood where they met numerous movieland icons such as Spencer Tracy, Groucho Marx, and Cary Grant. Life was good, although a new turn in Jack's baseball odyssey was about to take place…

18

An All-Star Season in South America

Jack was called upon between the 1955 and 1956 baseball seasons to play winter ball for the Caracas Magallanes baseball team in Venezuela. Jack and the family flew to Caracas and the South American adventure began. Lohrke, along with a few other former major leaguers, started for the Magallanes club and led them to a Venezuelan league championship.

After the season, the Magallanes qualified to play in the 1955 Caribbean Series against champions from Cuba, Panama, and Puerto Rico. Panama boasted the likes of two young stars, Roberto Clemente and Willie Mays!

The fabulous Roberto Clemente

Jack did so well that he was named to the Caribbean All-Star Team at the end of the series, after the Magallanes compiled a 4 and 2 series record, finishing in second. Jack teammates on the All-Star squad included Willie Mays, Sad Sam Jones, and Don Zimmer.

19

Go North Young Man

Dad and Kurt, 1956

Jack left the Stars and signed a contract with another team in the Pacific Coast League to play the 1956 season. Lohrke's new team would be the Seattle Rainiers, a quality club with fine coaches.

In '56, Jack was reunited with his old friend from the New York Giants, Larry Jansen, who was one of the Rainiers' coaches. A young teammate of Jack's in Seattle was future LA Dodger great Maury Wills.

Maury Wills

Jack was a part-time player for Seattle in 1956 and '57, and he would later move on to the Portland Beavers where he would become a player-coach in early 1958, as well as a coach for the Sacramento Solons at the end of the year.

20

The Last Innings

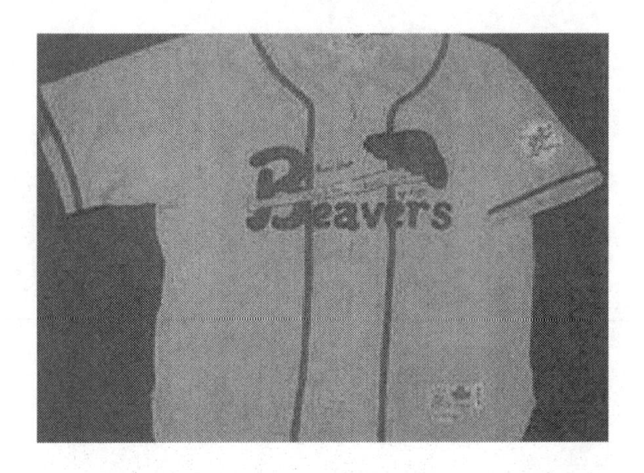

Lohrke would spend his last year in organized baseball in 1959 at the age of thirty-five as player-manager of Tri-Cities (Kennewick, Richland, and Pasco, Washington) in the Class B Northwest League (SABR, 2015).

During Jack's post-major league playing days in the Pacific Coast League, he ended up being a relief pitcher in addition to his service as a utility infielder. Jack had 25 pitching appearances (24 in relief) as he posted a respectable 2.35 ERA in 53⅓ innings (SABR, 2015). Leo Durocher's idea of converting Lucky to a pitcher finally came to fruition.

In 1960, the Major Leagues came calling to see if Jack would be interested in becoming a scout. With a growing family in Southern California (twins John and Kim were born in 1957) and a scout's starting salary being on the lower level, Jack decided to take the responsible route and turned down the Giants' inquiry.

21

Seasons of Security

He ended up getting hired by AeroJet General as a security officer in Sacramento, where the family relocated to start a new chapter in their lives. (In 1963, my beautiful bride, Kristina, the youngest of the Lohrke clan, was born!)

Jack Lohrke taking a rare break

Time moved forward and Jack ended up working for the government in the security field at Lawrence Livermore Laboratory. In 1974, he embarked upon a secret mission on the Glomar Explorer ship with a special Central Intelligence Agency team to search for a Soviet submarine that had been lost at sea.

The Glomar was built by Howard Hughes' shipbuilding company and was partially successful in the covert mission during the throes of the 1970's Cold War era. Nuclear codes and missiles were the catalyst for this secret mission which lasted many months.

The Glomar Explorer

In 1986, Jack Lohrke retired from the Lockheed Corporation, ending his many years of stellar service as captain of security. Even though he hadn't played baseball for almost thirty years, he continued to follow the exploits of the Giants, who were now based in San Francisco.

Along the way, his oldest child, Kurt, had starred on the baseball diamond at Santa Clara University. Kurt was drafted by the Boston Red Sox and played for a number of years in their minor league system, making it up to Triple-A. Jack's younger son, John, moved up to Alaska and became a general manager for a minor league squad. Even youngest daughter Kristina got into the act as she did the stats for the Foster City Giants, a local semi-pro baseball club.

O Lucky Man

A twist of fate saved Jack Lohrke from the worst tragedy in minor league history • by

I am the shadow sinister called Fate. . . . I am the Master Umpire and I call the plays the way I see them. I have raised my arm, and nine grand boys are out.

—SPOKANE INDIANS' MEMORIAL PROGRAM, July 8, 1946

Lohrke recalls the Indians as they were before the crash.

Shortly before 11 o'clock on the drizzly morning of Monday, June 24, 1946, 16 members of the Spokane Indian baseball team of the Class B Western International League boarded a chartered bus for Bremerton, 295 miles across Washington State. The players were in a jubilant humor, for though they were in only fifth place after 60 games, the day before they had rallied in the ninth inning to defeat the front-running Salem (Ore.) Senators in the second game of a doubleheader. The Indians were convinced their season was about to turn around.

Spokane was a solid ball club in a fast minor league made all the faster by the return of so many World War II veterans. After 40 games the Indians had five regulars hitting better than .300: third baseman Jack Lohrke, first baseman Vic Picetti, outfielder Levi McCormack, outfielder Bob Paterson and infielder-outfielder Fred Martinez. Then a brief slump dropped the team in the standings, but the players' confidence was unshaken. The Indians, in fact, had several bona fide big league prospects. Lohrke, a smooth fielder hitting .345 on June 24, was considered a solid bet, and so were the speedy Paterson (.317, 15 stolen bases) and Martinez (the team's leading hitter after 60 games, at .353). Lohrke and Paterson were 22, Martinez 24. All three were war veterans. Another vet, 24-year-old Milt Cadinha, a righthanded pitcher who, at only 5'10" and 160 pounds, was at least a long-shot prospect because of his hopping fastball, sharp curve and (at that level of play) unhittable screwball. Cadinha had an 8-1 record as the team bus left for Bremerton.

But the surefire major leaguer among the Indians, they all agreed, was Picetti, the latest in a line of San Francisco-bred Italian-American ballplayers that included the DiMaggio brothers, Frankie Crosetti and the 1941 National League MVP, Dolf Camilli. Picetti had attracted hordes of major league scouts as a star at San Francisco's Mission High School and at a national high school all-star game at the Polo Grounds, in New York City. But

Sports Illustrated wrote an article about Dad in 1994

22

Honors and Recognition

In 1997, Jack received a surprise phone call from the Bayview Raimondi Baseball Players Association, a group of retired Coast League players who honored PCL alumni.

Dad and the author at Francesco's, 1997

Kristina and I were honored to be the guests of Jack and Marie at the legendary Francesco's restaurant in Oakland to witness Jack's reception of a beautiful plaque commemorating his years in the Coast League.

Francesco's Restaurant
8520 PARDEE & HEGENBERGER ROAD
OAKLAND, CALIFORNIA 94621
510-569-0653

1997 COMMITTEE

1. RAY MALGRADI
2. JUG MANDISH
3. RAY ANTONALI
4. FRANK McCORMICK
5. SAM BERCOVICH
6. DEWEY BARGIACCHI

HONORED GUESTS

1. RON FIMRITE
2. JACK LOHRKE
3. JACKIE JONES
4. NICK BUSCOVICH

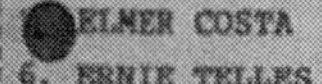

ELMER COSTA
6. ERNIE TELLES

DEWEY BARGIACCHI, CORDIALLY INVITES YOU TO THE
TWENTY THIRD BAYVIEW-RAIMONDI BASEBALL PLAYERS RE
TO BE HELD IN THE AIRPORT ROOM, SATURDAY, JUNE,7,
FULL COURSE LUNCHEON, CHOICE OF SIRLOIN STEAK OR
SOLE. PRICE PER PERSON: $17.00 NO HOST COCKTAILS
TO 1:00 P.M. LUNCH AT 1:30 P.M. FRIENDS AND RELA
ARE WELCOME.

EACH YEAR I PERSONALLY LOOK FORWARD TO THIS DA
REMINISCING WITH SOME OF MY OLD TEAM MATES AND TH
PLAYERS THAT I PLAYED AGAINST. WITHOUT A DOUBT, T
WILL BE ONE OF OUR GREATEST REUNIONS DUE TO THE A
ENTHUSIASM OF MY COMMITTEE.

I AM VERY PROUD OF THIS SPECIAL DAY KNOWING THA
IS THE ONLY ONE OF ITS KIND IN THE STATE OF CALIF
WHICH HONORS ITS FORMER AND PRESENT SEMI-PRO BAS
PLAYERS. AND FOR SURE YOU WILL SEE SOMEONE THAT
HAVE'NT SEEN IN YEARS. FOR ME THIS IS AN AFTERN
OF RELIVING PAST MEMORIES OF OUR BASEBALL DAYS A
WE PLAYED AT BAYVIEW, WASHINGTON AND LINCOLN PARK, BUSHROD, FRUITVALE DI
LOCKWOOD AND ELMHURST DIAMONDS. TALK ABOUT REMINISCING, I CAN REMEMBER L
TO CHARLIE TYE EACH SUNDAY NIGHT ON STATION K.L.X GIVING US A RUN DOWN ON
GAMES PLAYED. AND DO I MISS THE MONDAY NIGHT BASEBALL MEETINGS HELD AT T
McCLMONDS SCHOOL AUDITORIUM WITH ART MACY, SPARKY CORREIA, GEORGE GERICHT
AMBROSE DEL VECCHIO, MANUEL DUARTE, STEVE GRAHAM AND FRANK J. YOUELL WHO
THE OFFICERS OF OUR NORTHERN CALIFORNIA BASEBALL ASSOCIATION.

LOOKING FORWARD TO SEEING YOU ON SATURDAY, JUNE, 7, 1997, MAY GOD BLESS.

ARIVEDERCI,

Dewey

Jack and Marie's 50th wedding anniversary with the kids

Two years later, in 1999, the San Francisco Giants honored former Pacific Coast League players at Candlestick Park with an on-field ceremony. Jack was given one of the loudest bursts of applause when his name was announced and his image was shown on the jumbotron. Lucky was still a fan favorite forty years after he last laced up his spikes and roamed the infield!

Dad being honored at Candlestick Park in 1999

Handsome, as always, at Candlestick, 1999

23

The Greatest Reunion of the Greatest Team

In 2001, the San Francisco Giants invited members of the legendary 1951 New York Giants club to be honored at Pac Bell Park, the new home of the Giants, to commemorate the 50th anniversary of the famous "Shot Heard 'Round the World." (Sadly, the reunion was postponed because of the 9/11 terrorist attacks on the East Coast, consequently the memorable affair was held in 2002.)

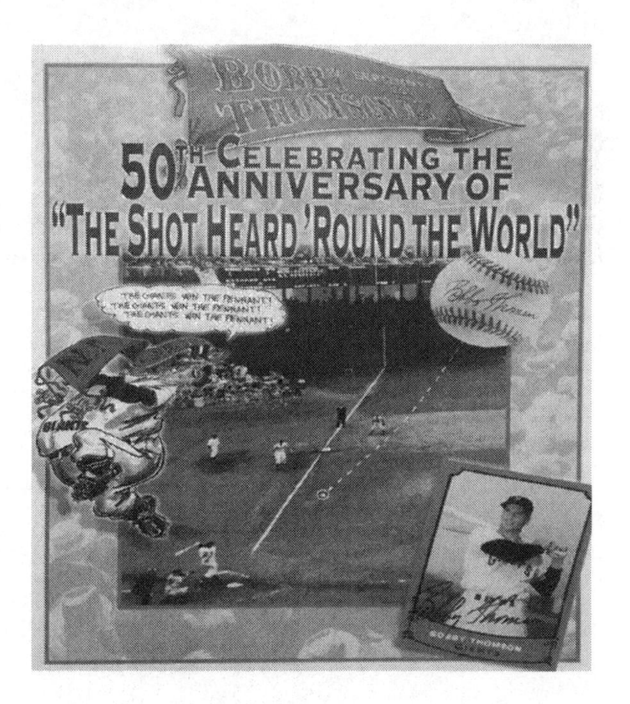

Once again, Kristina and I were blessed to be the guests of Jack and Marie. In a surreal day, we had lunch at the ballpark's Chophouse restaurant with legends Lon Simmons, Whitey Lockman, Alvin Dark, Bobby Thomson, Don Mueller, Al Corwin, Larry Jansen, and other members of the '51 Giants team. The stories were amazing, the food was good, and the company was superlative.

Mom and Dad looking as great as ever!

I was able to chat with numerous players and upon my return to my seat, I was greeted by the burly Lon Simmons, who was chatting with Kristina. In his low and oh so familiar voice, Lon stated bluntly, "Well, I'm not sure what you'll be doing later today, but I'll be out on a date with this lovely lady!"

The legendary Lon Simmons!

“The Scot” and his teammates celebrate the ‘51 pennant

In 2002, I truly believe the magic of having the New York Giants' family at the ballpark that day was one of the reasons why SF won the pennant that fall, as they moved on to the Series against the LA Angels.

Oh so close, in 2002, against the Angels...

Two years later, in 2004, another reunion took place at the Giants ballpark as team management called upon members of the 1954 World Championship New York Giants squad to come together for a 50th reunion. Jack and Marie were invited by his longtime friend, Whitey Lockman, even though Jack didn't play for the team in '54. We were very fortunate to accompany Jack and Marie as their guests for this wonderful event. We got to meet Monte Irvin, Joe Garagiola, Dusty Rhodes, John Antonelli, and many other World Series alumni and baseball people from 1954. It was a truly memorable night!

Mom and Dad with the "Carolina Comet", Whitey Lockman

24

A Return to the Diamond

In 2008, I thought I would give baseball another try after many years of wondering what might have been, so I did the next best thing for a forty-four year old: I signed up for a slow-pitch softball team. I ended up getting shelled in my first game as the "Ten Most Wanted" starting pitcher, but after many games I learned how to pitch and even got a few hits.

I would recant some of the games' events to my father-in-law, getting him to laugh a bit at my somewhat athletic anecdotes. Just being able to chat with Dad over the years was something I will always cherish, especially our conversations as we drove to our monthly barber appointments over the hill to Livermore to visit local barber legend and sports fan John Locatelli.

The "baseball odyssey" of Jack Lohrke was an amazing tale of talent, perseverance, and success. This American hero and baseball legend will never be forgotten!

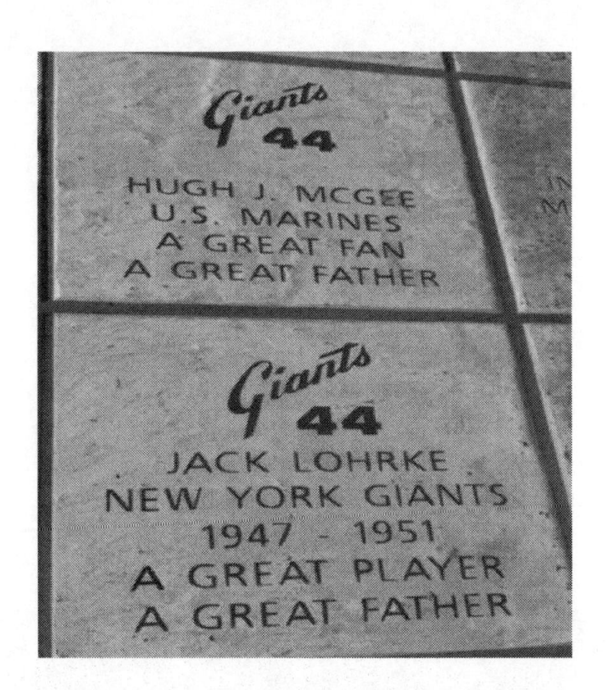

Dad was inducted into the Hall of Champions

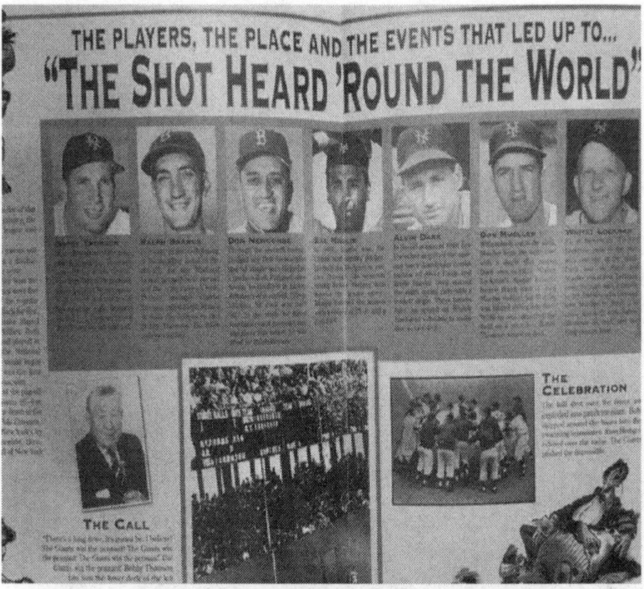

THE PLAYERS, THE PLACE AND THE EVENTS THAT LED UP TO...

"THE SHOT HEARD 'ROUND THE WORLD"

THE CALL

THE CELEBRATION

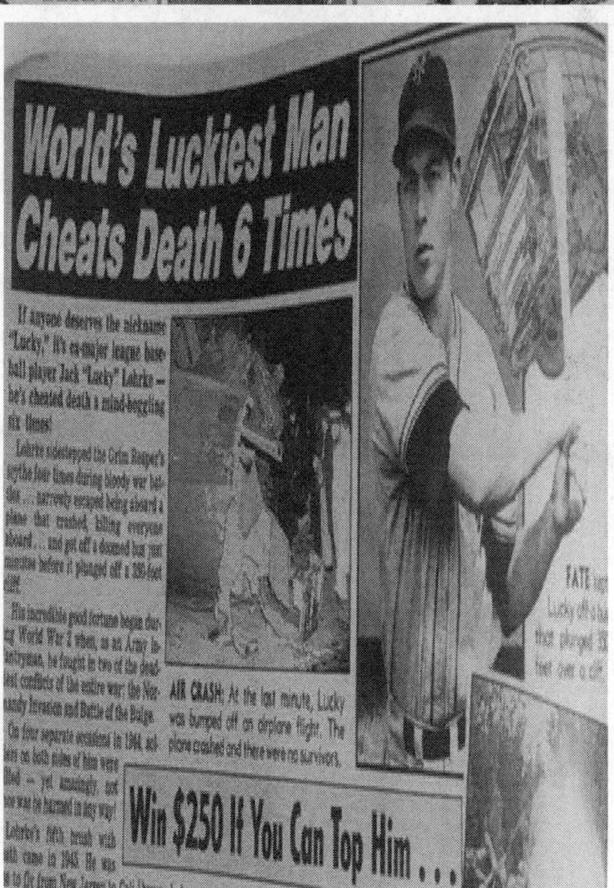

World's Luckiest Man Cheats Death 6 Times

If anyone deserves the nickname "Lucky," it's ex-major league baseball player Jack "Lucky" Lohrke — he's cheated death a mind-boggling six times!

Lohrke sidestepped the Grim Reaper's scythe four times during bloody war battles . . . narrowly escaped being aboard a plane that crashed, killing everyone aboard . . . and got off a doomed bus just minutes before it plunged off a 350-foot cliff.

His incredible good fortune began during World War 2 when, as an Army infantryman, he fought in two of the deadliest conflicts of the entire war: the Normandy Invasion and Battle of the Bulge.

On four separate occasions in 1944, soldiers on both sides of him were killed — yet amazingly, not one was he harmed in any way!

Lohrke's fifth brush with death came in 1945. He was ... to fly from New Jersey to Cali...

AIR CRASH: At the last minute, Lucky was bumped off an airplane flight. The plane crashed and there were no survivors.

Win $250 If You Can Top Him . . .

FRANCESCO'S
JACK LOHRKE

Sources

Sturgill, Andy, SABR (Society of Baseball Research), 2010

Google Images, 2019

Made in the USA
San Bernardino, CA
20 February 2020